Dad Jokes

Assault With A Dad-ly Weapon

Elias Hill

Illustrations By:
Katherine Hogan

DEDICATION

To all the dads we wish we could hear
one more joke from.

How do you know if you have a severe iron deficiency?

Your shirt will be all wrinkled.

I don't usually make bad puns about fractions.

But I will if I halve two.

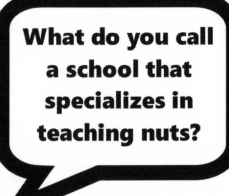

I taught my son how to use the word "abundance" in a sentence.

He said, "Thanks, Dad, that really means a lot."

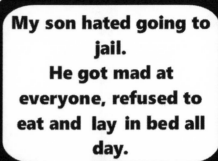

I need to call the doctor today.

Which doctor?

No, the regular kind.

My wife just bought me a chicken and an egg off Amazon.

I'll let you know which comes first.

I can always tell when someone is lying.

I can also tell when they're standing.

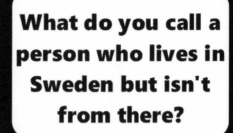

Yesterday, I crossed a road, changed a light bulb and walked into a bar.

My life is turning into a joke.

How long should a jousting match last?

Until knight fall.

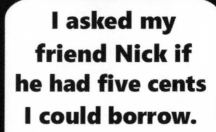

I asked my friend Nick if he had five cents I could borrow.

But he was Nicholas.

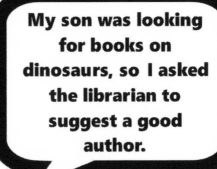

I don't like to brag about how all my friends let me borrow their brass instruments.
I just don't want to toot my own horn.

I feel bad for deep-sea fish.

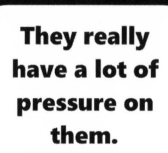

They really have a lot of pressure on them.

My coworkers are like my Christmas lights.

Half of them don't work, and the other half aren't that bright.

Son, how can I stop my dad jokes?

Whatever means necessary.

Ha, no it doesn't!

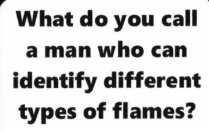

I removed the shell from my favorite racing snail thinking it would make him faster.

But it's actually made him more sluggish.

You know what I've always said about suspense...

What happened when the pig fell off his horse?

He got ba-con, of course.

My wife asked if our kids were spoiled.

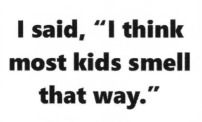

I said, "I think most kids smell that way."

A rude banker wouldn't stop making fun of me.

So I asked him to just leave me a loan.

I'm allergic to green onions.

Every time I eat them, I break out in chives.

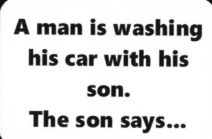

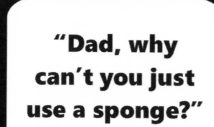

My friend said, "I need to go and feed my baby guinea pigs."

I said, "Are you sure your baby will like them?"

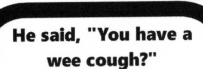

Can you make puns about Mediterranean islands?

Of Corsican, don't be Sicily!

You, wanna hear a joke about someone who never goes outdoors?
Actually, you wouldn't get it. It's an inside joke.

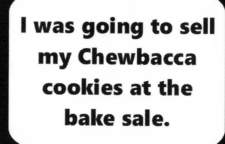

I was going to sell my Chewbacca cookies at the bake sale.

But they were all a little Chewy.

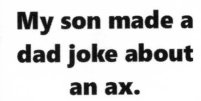

My son made a dad joke about an ax.

But it just wasn't very cleaver.

We can't take our dog outside anymore because the ducks keep attacking him.

Guess that's what we get for buying a pure bread dog.

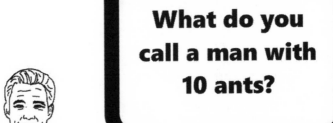

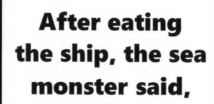

After eating the ship, the sea monster said,

"I can't believe I ate the hull thing."

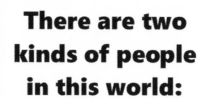

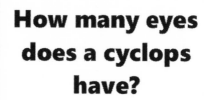

How many eyes does a cyclops have?

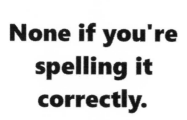

None if you're spelling it correctly.

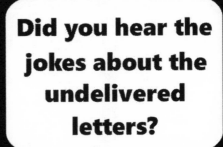

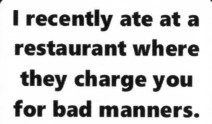

Scary monsters aren't very good at math.

Unless you Count Dracula.

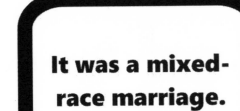

Other Dad Jokes Books You Might Enjoy!